Sister Jennie has a treat for you:

To enjoy

a Shaker Plum Pudding is to share the pleasure of a bountiful dinner table in a family dwelling house of long ago.

To sample

the hearty texture of Sister Jennie's "Cocoa Nut Cake" is to learn how bland the modern cake has become.

To taste

authentic Shaker mince pie is to find that dining with the Believers could rise far above the level of simple utilitarianism.

The recipes in this book come from a private notebook kept for many years by a Shaker sister. All the recipes have been thoroughly tested and edited for easy use by modern cooks. Both the modern recipes and Sister Jennie's originals in her own handwriting appear in **Sister Jennie's Shaker Desserts**

sister Jennie M Wells

Sister Jennie's Shaker Desserts

by
Arthur Tolve and James Bissland III

Design by Lynn Hostetler

Photography by Frank Breithaupt

Gabriel's Horn  Publishing Co.
Bowling Green, Ohio

An invitation

Your comments on this book, including suggestions for its im-
provement in later editions, are welcome. So are any questions you
might have. The authors would also like to know if you would like
them to publish more of Sister Jennie's desserts, or other Shaker
recipes. Write the authors in care of *Gabriel's Horn Publishing Co.*,
P.O. Box 141, Bowling Green, Ohio 43402.

Contents

Shaker Memories

A reminiscence by James Bissland III

When I was a boy in the 1940s, my parents and I would often climb into one of the old cars Dad favored in those days and thread our way through the Berkshire Hills of western Massachusetts to visit the Shakers. For a while we traveled to Mt. Lebanon, N.Y., but when that society closed and its elderly refugees moved a few miles east to join another handful of Believers remaining near Pittsfield, Mass., we followed. Today, the Shakers are gone from Pittsfield too, but their former home is the beautifully restored Hancock Shaker Village, a public museum.

It was not a museum then; it was a living society, though sadly diminished in its membership and activity. The Shakers there gave me a host of indulgent great aunts and grandparents. They did more for my father: with tongues only slightly in cheek, they dubbed him Brother James and entrusted to his guardianship the beloved North Family mascot, an enormous, ancient tiger cat named Moses, to whom they mailed homemade Christmas cards thereafter.

Among our Shaker friends in those days was a sprightly little sister, with a no-nonsense air about her, named Jennie M. Wells. Sister Jennie gave my father a small, leatherbound notebook into which, over many years, she had entered her favorite recipes. It is selections from that notebook's array of desserts that you will find in the publication in your hand. These are not fancy recipes; they are Shaker, simple and good. When Dad was first getting acquainted with the Shakers and learning their ways, he wrote Sister Jennie to confirm some tale he had heard about Shakers making French or puff pastry. "We never went in for such fancy cooking," Jennie snorted in reply. "In ye olden times it would not be allowed. Our cooking was plain and wholesome."

Publishing some of these recipes is a way of remembering my late father, who loved the Shakers, and Sister Jennie, who regularly began her letters to him with "My dear boy...." I hope you enjoy the recipes. Like Sister Jennie and the Shakers, they are plain and wholesome, simple and good.

Tasting the Shaker Past

An introduction by Arthur Tolve

These recipes offer more than a variety of tempting desserts. They offer an opportunity to travel backward through time and to experience part of the Shaker past by dining on cakes, pies, gingerbread, cookies and pudding that taste just as they did to Believers decades ago. To enjoy a Shaker plum pudding is to share some of the pleasure of a bountiful dinner table in a family dwelling house of long ago. To sample the hearty texture of Sister Jennie's "Cocoa Nut Cake" is to learn something about how bland the modern cake has become. And anyone fortunate enough to taste authentic Shaker mince pie will find that dining with the Believers could rise far above the level of simple utilitarianism.

As someone who has spent a professional lifetime in the kitchen or nearby one, I consider Sister Jennie's little manuscript recipe book an exciting find. It is a set of messages from somebody of another time...and an opportunity to share the experience of making food much as it was made long ago.

Bringing Sister Jennie's recipes to life again was not a simple task, however. Jotted down over many years, her recipes often consist only of lists of ingredients, without directions. A few ingredients have no direct counterpart in modern stores. And the measurements used by Sister Jennie do not correspond with our modern measuring system. She knew what she meant when she referred to "cups," "tablespoons," and so forth, but we do not.

And so it was necessary to engage in some "kitchen archaeology," to reconstruct the tastes of the past from incomplete evidence. Into this happy task went nearly eight months of experimenting and testing, of reformulating ingredients and rewriting Sister Jennie's recipes in language for the modern cook. Students in the test kitchens of Bowling Green State University, neighbors, families and friends, all were drawn into the job. Now it is your turn. *You are cordially invited to try these recipes and to let us know what you think by writing the authors in care of the publisher.*

Suggestions for Success

Ingredients: Always use the freshest, purest ingredients; they are vital to achieving the authentic, natural flavors of Sister Jennie's desserts. Of course, it is not possible today to precisely duplicate every ingredient from an earlier, simpler age. For example, we cannot obtain the same thick, heavy (and unpasteurized!) cream direct from the dairy barn that Sister Jennie could. Nevertheless, even today we can come quite close through careful shopping at good, large supermarkets. In testing our recipes we did find that light coffee or "medium" cream should be used in those recipes where *cream* is specified; heavy cream need be used only where we so indicate. For *butter*, sweet, unsalted butter should be obtained. Do not substitute margarine! Furthermore, "tub butter" will produce the finest flavored results. For *flour*, light, delicate cake flour should be employed for cakes, and heavier, full-bodied all-purpose flour for other recipes. Do not use self-rising flour unless the recipe calls for it. The *vanilla extract* you use should be pure and natural, not imitation. The *baking powder* we used in testing Sister Jennie's recipes was double acting. This product gave consistent results.

Measurements: Use the same set of standardized measuring instruments every time you bake a recipe in order to achieve consistent quality. Remember, too, there are measuring instruments specifically for use with dry ingredients, and those specifically for liquid ingredients. For *dry ingredients*, be sure your measurements are level. Heaped ingredients should be leveled with the edge of a cake spatula. *Liquid ingredients* require the utmost accuracy; the liquid in a measuring utensil should appear to be resting on the utensil's measuring line.

Flour should always be sifted *before* measuring. It can be sifted directly into the measuring utensil or heaped in afterwards with a spatula, but in either case be sure to level the flour with the edge of a spatula. Do not shake the sifted flour while measuring or the air incorporated in it during sifting will be lost. *Granulated sugar*, if lumpy, should be sifted before measuring, but *brown sugar* should be packed firmly into the dry measuring utensil to remove air pockets and then leveled with the edge of a spatula. Because *syrups and frostings* are thick and viscous and tend to heap in the center of the utensil, level them off evenly after heaping in a dry measuring utensil. *Oils* should be poured into liquid measuring utensils, with care taken that the measurement is level and even. Melted butter should also be measured in this manner. Be sure to scrape the side of the measuring utensil to remove any clinging oil. *Eggs,* when used singly, should be of large size. With quantities, measure the eggs in liquid measuring cupfuls, counting each cupful as the equivalent of 4 extra-large eggs, or 5 large eggs, or 6 medium eggs, or 7 small eggs.

Preparation Method for Butter Cakes: Be sure to grease cake pans and dust them lightly with flour before filling. Do not fill pans more than 3/4 full of batter. Drop the filled pans a few times, lightly, on the work surface to remove any air pockets that might produce tunneling. Spread the batter to the edges of the pans so it is thicker at the edges than at the center. This will result in an even cake. Generally, 360°F to 375°F may be used for thinner cakes, while 340°F to 350°F will produce the best results for loaves and thicker cakes.

When done, butter cakes: (1) are evenly brown, with firm-looking crusts; (2) draw away from the sides of the pan; (3) spring back when the tops are pressed lightly with the finger; (4) have no sound of cooking batter when held 4 or 5 inches from the ear; (5) allow a dry toothpick, inserted at the center of the cake, to come out clean. Butter cakes should remain in the pans for 2 or 3 minutes after being taken from the oven. They should then be inverted and removed to a wire cake rack to cool before frosting.

Preparation Method for Sponge Cakes: Use 9″ or 10″ tube pans or 12″ by 17″ jelly roll pans. Do not grease or flour the pans. Carefully cut through the batter with a cake spatula to remove any trapped air that might cause tunneling. Do not drop these cakes! Most sponge cakes bake best at 325°F to 350°F and take longer than butter cakes.

When done, sponge cakes: (1) are lighter in color than butter cakes; (2) are light in texture; (3) are light in weight for their size; (4) do not have a thick, sugary, gummy crust; (5) spring back when depressed with the finger; (6) separate slightly from the side of the pan.

Sponge cakes should be cooled in the pans, inverted and suspended so the surface of the cake does not touch the rack. Remove sponge cakes from their pans only when *cold.*

Sister Jennie's Coconut Cake is flanked by a Shaker oval box of her cupcakes with boiled frosting.

Cake

Recipes for cake were the most popular of all with Sister Jennie; they constitute more than half her manuscript's array of desserts. Perhaps this reflects the surge of interest in cake baking in America during the second half of the 19th century following the discovery of baking powder. Until then, cooks had needed hours of hand beating in order to trap sufficient air in the cake batter to raise it. Here are just some of Sister Jennie's favorite cake recipes: butter cakes, sponge cakes and frosting.

Cocoa Nut Cake

Cocoanut	1 lb
Sugar	1 lb
Flour	3 cups
Eggs	8
Cream sweet	2 cups
Baking powder	2 teaspons

Coconut Cake

Sister Jennie's "Cocoa Nut Cake" is light, tender and moist, and it was an instant hit with our test panels. Its hearty texture is a welcome contrast to the bland body of the typical modern cake. You can bake Sister Jennie's Coconut Cake in tube pans, *or* bake it in a jelly roll pan, spread it with ice cream, then roll and freeze it until needed.

4 eggs, separated
1/8 teaspoon cream of tartar
1/2 cup sugar
1/4 cup sugar
8-oz. package shredded coconut

1 1/2 cups cake flour
1 teaspoon baking powder
1 teaspoon vanilla extract
1 cup heavy cream
    warmed to 100°F

1. Beat the egg whites with the cream of tartar until soft peaks are formed.   **2.** Beat the 1/2 cup of sugar into the separated egg whites, a little at a time, to make a meringue that is stiff but not dry.   **3.** Beat egg yolks until lemon-colored and frothy.   **4.** Beat the 1/4 cup of sugar into the yolks, slowly, to retain the incorporated air, until light and lemon colored.   **5.** Combine the remaining dry ingredients, and fold into the meringue.   **6.** Fold the beaten yolks into the meringue next.   **7.** Mix flavoring with cream and fold in last.   **8.** Bake in an 8″ tube pan at 350°F for about 40 minutes. Follow the preparation method for sponge cakes (page 9).   **9.** Boiled Frosting (page 27) with shredded coconut on top is great with this cake, or you may prefer the ice cream roll version, described above.

Raised Cake

Set sponge with 1 qt new milk
in the morning add 1 qt cream, warm
sponge with small sloop of flour and
let rise till light, then add
3 lbs sugar
1 " butter & enough flour for thick
batter. When thoroughly light
stir in 3 lb. raisins & a little soda.
Bake in moderate oven 45 min.
or an hour.

Raised Cake

A bread-like texture characterizes Sister Jennie's Raised Cake. It is excellent for french toast, or browned in a toaster, or buttered, then sprinkled with cinnamon and sugar and toasted in an oven. Sister Jennie's Raised Cake may also be used as a basis for bread puddings, and it even makes a great cream-cheese-and-jelly sandwich!

1 cup milk
1 cup light cream
1 1/4 cups sugar
1/2 cup butter
1 envelope (1 tablespoon) dry
   activated yeast

1 tablespoon sugar
2 cups raisins
1/4 teaspoon soda
3 to 4 cups sifted all-purpose
   flour
1 teaspoon lemon rind

1. Have all ingredients at room temperature.   **2.** Heat milk to scalding.   **3.** Reserve 1/4 cup milk and beat in cream, sugar and butter to the remainder. Cool to 90°F.   **4.** Cool reserved milk, and when 110°F stir in yeast and the 1 tablespoon of sugar.   **5.** Let activate in a warm place, covered with a damp towel, for about 10 minutes, until frothy.   **6.** When cream mixture reaches 90°F, add activated yeast mixture, raisins, soda, rind and flour to make stiff batter.   **7.** Beat well. Cover with a damp towel.   **8.** Place in an off oven with a pilot light (a pan of hot water can substitute for a pilot light) and let rise until double in bulk.   **9.** Stir mixture to renew yeast activity.   **10.** Pour into greased and floured baking pans (loaf size 8″ by 4″ is perfect for this) until half full, and let rise again until double in bulk.   **11.** Place in 360°F oven and bake 45 minutes to 1 hour, until golden brown on top and a toothpick inserted at the center comes out clean.   **12.** Brush top with melted butter or warm milk when 3/4 done, if desired, to increase tenderness and enhance color.

If using larger pans, such as 9″ by 5″ loaf pans, this cake may take longer to bake. Reduce heat after 35 minutes and bake at 340°F for 15 to 20 minutes more.

Cup Cake

1 cup butter
2 " sugar
3 " flour
4 " eggs
3 moderate spoons Baking P.
6 cups flour. 3 cups sugar
6 eggs   1 " butter, 1 cup cream
6 teaspoons Baking Powder

Cupcakes

One way early American cooks remembered recipes was by using whole numbers for quantities of ingredients, as much as possible, and by arranging those quantities in a 1, 2, 3, 4 format, as Sister Jennie almost exactly did on the opposite page. Our version of Sister Jennie's cupcake recipe is not very different from the one jotted down in her little notebook.

Vanilla Cupcakes

1 cup butter	3 cups cake flour
1 teaspoon pure vanilla	3 teaspoons baking powder
1 1/2 cups sugar	1 teaspoon salt
4 eggs	

1. Cream the fat.   **2.** Add the flavoring and cream again.   **3.** Cream in sugar a little at a time.   **4.** Cream in eggs, one at a time.   **5.** Sift flour, baking powder and salt together, twice.   **6.** Divide flour mixture into four parts and add to creamed mixture, one part at a time. Do not beat while adding flour, just stir quickly. If fruit or nuts are to be added for variety, stir them in last.   **7.** Place spoonfuls of batter in muffin tins, being careful to fill them no more than 2/3 full. Be sure to grease and flour the muffin cups first, or line them with ungreased paper liners.   **8.** Bake at 375°F for about 12 to 15 minutes. This recipe makes about 12 medium-size cupcakes.

Chocolate Cupcakes: Use 2 cups all-purpose flour, instead of 3 cups of cake flour. Add 1 cup of cocoa to flour and sift 3 times before using. Reduce oven temperature to 360°F after 15 minutes and bake 10 minutes more.

Spice Cupcakes: To the 3 cups of flour, sift in 1 teaspoon cinnamon; 1/4 teaspoon each of cloves, allspice, and nutmeg; and 1/16 teaspoon black pepper.

Mocha-Spice Cupcakes: Sift together 2 cups all-purpose flour, 1 cup cocoa, 1 teaspoon each of cinnamon and instant coffee, 1/4 teaspoon each of cloves, allspice and nutmeg.

Layer Cake

2 cups flour
1 " sugar
1½ " milk
2 tablespoon butter
yolks of two eggs
whites of one "
2 teaspoons baking powder
Flavor with vanilla or lemon

Layer Cake

The popularity of layer cakes has increased in America partly because of modern packaged mixes offering ease of preparation. But Sister Jennie's recipe for layer cake is not only easily prepared, it permits you to create your own "convenience mix" for later use.

2 cups cake flour
1 cup sugar
2 teaspoons baking powder
1/2 teaspoon salt

1/4 cup butter
2 egg yolks, 1 egg white
1/2 cup milk or cream
1 teaspoon pure vanilla

1. Be sure all ingredients are at room temperature before starting preparation.   **2.** Sift flour, sugar, baking powder and salt together twice.   **3.** Cut the butter into the combined dry ingredients.   **4.** Mix eggs with milk and flavoring.   **5.** Add the liquid ingredients to the dry mixture, all at once.   **6.** Stir to combine well, but *do not beat*.   **7.** Follow preparation methods for making butter cakes (page 9). Bake 20 to 25 minutes at 360-375°F. This recipe makes one 9″ layer or fills one square pan 8″ x 8″ by 2″ deep.

You can make a hit with this cake by using homemade jam or a fine marmalade as a filling between the layers, and topping it all with Sister Jennie's Boiled Frosting or our Chocolate Powdered Sugar Frosting (page 27).

Convenience Mix: The dry mix (steps 1, 2 and 3, above) may be prepared and then stored in a refrigerator for up to 2 months before using. The modern package mix is not really such a new idea; the Shakers and other people of the 19th century used mixes too.

Custard Cake

1½ cup of flour
1 "   sugar
1 "   butter
3 "   eggs
1½ teaspoons Baking powder
bake in 4 loaves

Custard for Cake

1/2 pint milk
1/2 cup sugar
1/4 " corn starch
1 egg
1 tea spoon vanilla
spread between cake when cool

Custard Cake

Sister Jennie's Custard Cake offers a delicious change of pace from the traditional combinations of cake and frosting. It offers a choice of ways to combine the custard with cake too.

1 cup butter
1 teaspoon pure vanilla
1 cup sugar
3 eggs

2 cups cake flour
1 1/2 teaspoons baking powder
1/2 teaspoon salt

1. Cream the butter.   **2.** Add the flavoring and cream again.   **3.** Cream in the sugar, a little at a time.   **4.** Cream in the eggs, one at a time.   **5.** Sift flour, baking powder and salt together, twice.   **6.** Divide flour mixture into four parts.   **7.** Add flour mixture to creamed mixture, one part at time, stirring after each addition. Do not beat while adding flour, just stir quickly.   **8.** Follow preparation method for making butter cakes (page 9). Bake in four small loaves for 20 to 25 minutes at 360-375°F.   **9.** Serve covered with custard as a sauce, or split the loaves horizontally and fill between the layers with custard. Top with boiled frosting (page 27).

Custard for Cake

1/2 cup sugar
1/4 cup cornstarch
1/4 teaspoon salt
3/4 cup cold milk

1/4 cups scalded milk
2 eggs
2 teaspoons pure vanilla extract

1. Mix sugar, cornstarch and salt together, then add cold milk, stirring constantly.   **2.** Pour mixture into hot scalded milk over hot water in a double boiler, stirring constantly until thickened.   **3.** Beat in eggs, then cook 5 minutes more over low heat.   **4.** Beat in vanilla and allow to cool.

White Mountain Cake

3½ cups flour
2 " sugar
1 " milk
½ " butter
2 eggs
3 tea spoons Baking powder
Good for layer or loaf.

White Mountain Cake

This cake was popular with diners before the turn of the century. When baked in a loaf pan and topped with Boiled Frosting, the snowy mountain-like peak in the center of the cake draws interest, giving the cake its name.

3 1/2 cups flour
2 cups sugar
3 teaspoons baking powder
1 teaspoon salt

1/2 cup butter
2 eggs
1 cup milk
2 teaspoons pure vanilla

1. Sift dry ingredients together twice, into a mixing bowl.   **2.** Add butter that is soft enough to mix easily with dry ingredients. Stir carefully but thoroughly to combine well.   **3.** Add unbeaten eggs, one at a time, and stir after each addition.   **4.** Add combined milk and vanilla all at once, and stir to mix thoroughly.   **5.** Follow preparation method for butter cakes (page 9). Bake 20 to 25 minutes at 340-350°F; 360-375°F if baking in layers.   **6.** If cake is baked in layers, apply Boiled Frosting (page 27) between the layers as well as on top of the cake. Loaf cakes need only be frosted on top. Coconut may be added to the frosting to enhance the snowy effect.

Sponge Cake

5 eggs
1 cup flour
1 " sugar
 Flavor
Bake in moderate oven

Sponge Cake

Sister Jennie collected no fewer than *five* recipes for sponge cake in her little book, but this one is our favorite. Because it contains no baking powder, it is a true sponge cake. It can also be made into a jelly roll.

1 cup sugar
5 eggs, separated
1 cup sifted cake flour

1/4 teaspoon salt
1 teaspoon pure vanilla

1. Heat sugar in a shallow pan in a 350°F oven until it is very warm, but has not darkened in color.   **2.** Beat egg yolks until frothy and add half the heated sugar, a little at a time, beating constantly while adding.   **3.** When mixture is lemon-colored, fluffy and cool, fold in flour carefully, a little at a time, to form a batter. *Do not beat at this time.*   **4.** Beat egg whites until soft peaks are formed. Beat in the other half of the heated sugar, a little at a time, to form a meringue.   **5.** Fold the meringue into the batter. *Do not beat either during or after folding.*   **6.** Follow preparation method for sponge cakes (page 9), baking 35 to 45 minutes at 325-350°F.

When making jelly rolls from sponge cake recipes, follow the preparation method for sponge cake but line the bottom of the pan with waxed paper. Bake in a moderate oven for 7 to 10 minutes; remove before browned. Quickly loosen sides with the cutting edge of a spatula, being careful not to tear the sponge. Invert the cake onto a damp towel that has been sprinkled liberally with granulated sugar. Roll up the sponge in the towel. Allow to cool. When cooled, unroll, spread with jam or marmalade, and re-roll to slice.

Boiled Frosting

1 cup gran. sugar 3 tablespoons water
boil till clear. — pour on white of beaten
egg, stirring till cold, This makes enough
for three good sized cakes.

Boiled Frosting

Sister Jennie's Boiled Frosting makes an attractive and tasty topping for many of her cakes. For variety, we also include here our Chocolate Powdered Sugar Frosting.

Boiled Frosting

2 egg whites
1/8 teaspoon cream of tartar
1/3 cup water

1 cup granulated sugar
1 teaspoon pure vanilla

1. Beat 2 egg whites with 1/8 teaspoon cream of tartar until soft peaks are formed.   **2.** Heat 1/3 cup water to boiling, then add 1 cup granulated sugar. Cook 5 minutes without stirring. The sugar and water should be cooked to the "thread stage"; that is, until the mixture spins a two-inch thread when dropped from a fork or spoon. It is also 230°F at sea level.   **3.** Pour the hot syrup over the beaten whites in a thin stream, beating constantly until cool.   **4.** Beat in 1 teaspoon pure vanilla. This recipe makes a generous cupful, enough for the top of one 9″ two-layer cake.

Chocolate Powdered Sugar Frosting

3 1/2 cups powdered sugar
1/4 cup heavy cream
3 tablespoons butter

1 square of chocolate
2 teaspoons vanilla

1. To 3 1/2 cups sifted powdered sugar, stir in 1/4 cup heavy cream, warmed.   **2.** Melt 3 tablespoons butter with 1 square unsweetened chocolate and beat into sugar-and-cream mixture until soft and creamy.   **3.** Beat in 2 teaspoons vanilla. Use at once.

Sister Jennie's "Plain Cookies" are neither plain to taste or look at, especially when embossed with cookie stamps carved from potatoes, as these were (foregound).

Cookies

Cookies are really little cakes; most butter cake recipes can be modified to produce cookies merely by reducing the liquid. Cookies were a great favorite with Shaker field hands, for quantities of them could be easily carried, kept without difficulty in a round wooden lunch pail and drawn on from time to time to "fill in the chinks" that developed between mealtimes. Sister Jennie's own favorites included her "Plain Cookies" and her potent Gingersnaps.

Plain Cookies

6 cups flour
3 " sugar
1 " butter
1 " sour cream
3 eggs
1½ teaspoon's soda

Plain Cookies

What Sister Jennie called her "Plain Cookies" have a delicate flavor that makes them delicious to eat, and—if you imprint them with your own cookie stamps made the old-fashioned way—fun to look at, too.

1/2 cup butter	3/4 teaspoon soda
2 teaspoons flavoring extract	1 teaspoon salt
1 1/2 cups sugar	1/2 cup sour cream
2 eggs	4 cups cake flour, variable

1. Cream the butter and flavoring.   **2.** Add the sugar a little at a time, creaming well after each addition.   **3.** Add eggs one at a time, and cream well after each addition.   **4.** Mix the soda and salt with the sour cream, and add this mixture to the creamed mixture, alternately with the flour: four parts of flour to three parts of sour cream.   **5.** Roll out the dough and press with the tines of a fork or, if you wish, with cookie stamps you make yourself, as explained below.   **6.** Cut the cookies into the desired shapes. Roll the dough, 1/8" thick, in a greased jelly roll pan, then stamp the designs and cut out strips between the designs to form squares. These may be baked right in the pan without bothering to move and re-position them.   **7.** Bake at 375°F for 8 to 10 minutes. This recipe makes about 8 dozen cookies. (These cookies are especially tasty when sprinkled with a mixture of 1 tablespoon of cinnamon and 1 cup of sugar when the cookies are hot from the oven.)

Homemade Cookie Stamps: Stamps can be made from potatoes, carrots or turnips. Cut the vegetable to provide a flat surface of the size needed for your design. Use a paring knife to carve the desired design into the flat surface. Dust the stamp with powdered sugar or flour before using.

Ginger Snaps

1 cup butter
1 "   sugar
1 "   molasses.
1 table spoon ginger
Flour must be worked in till
stiff enough to roll.

Gingersnaps

Here are cookies with character. Like Shaker doctrine, they deserve respect; Sister Jennie's crisp and spicy gingersnaps are not for the timid.

1 cup butter
1 cup sugar
1 1/3 cups molasses
2 tablespoons ginger

5 to 6 cups sifted all-purpose flour
1 teaspoon salt
1/2 teaspoon baking soda

1. Cream the butter.   **2.** Add sugar a little at a time, creaming well after each addition.   **3.** Add molasses slowly and continue beating until mixture is light and creamy.   **4.** Mix salt and soda with flour and add to creamed mixture a little at a time, stirring vigorously.   **5.** Add enough flour to make a dough that may be rolled easily.   **6.** Roll the dough on a floured board and cut with small round cutters.   **7.** Grease cookie sheet and bake at 400°F for 5 to 8 minutes. *Do not overbake, as gingersnaps burn easily.* This recipe makes 6 dozen small cookies.

Be sure to enjoy these cookies with a tall glass of cold milk. Or try this: Crush the cookies with a rolling pin and spread over hot oatmeal sprinkled with brown sugar. You can also sprinkle the crushed cookies on ice cream, plain puddings, or on whipped cream on pies. When thoroughly crushed, gingersnaps also may be used instead of graham cracker crumbs for a pie crust, or even instead of flour to thicken pot roast gravy!

Boiled frosting is just one way to enhance Sister Jennie's Soft Gingerbread, shown here with a Shaker apple tray.

Gingerbread

Although it is basically a cake, with molasses and spices added, gingerbread seems to have had a special appeal of its own to the people of Sister Jennie's time. Her recipe book included a number of variations. With its spicy aroma, gingerbread baking in the ovens of Shaker woodstoves must have brightened many autumn days in the dwelling houses of the Believers.

Soft Gingerbread

Rule C. J. M. brought from
Pittsfield

1 cup sugar
½ " butter
1 " molasses
2 eggs
1 teaspoonful ginger
1 " " cinnamon
½ nutmeg
1 teaspoon soda dissolved in
1 cup boiling water
2 teacups of flour.

Soft Gingerbread

This is the answer to a gingerbread lover's dream. Sister Jennie noted that it was the "rule C.J.M. brought from Pittsfield" (a western Massachusetts city near the Shaker societies at Hancock and Mt. Lebanon). We do not know who C.J.M. was; perhaps she was a Shaker sister who brought this and other recipes with her when she joined the Believers.

1/2 cup butter
1 cup sugar
1 cup molasses
2 1/2 cups all-purpose flour
1 teaspoon each: ginger,
    cinnamon, nutmeg

1/2 teaspoon salt
1 teaspoon soda, dissolved in...
1 cup boiling water
2 eggs

1. Cream the butter. **2.** Add sugar a little at a time, creaming well after each addition. **3.** Add molasses slowly and continue beating until mixture is light and creamy. **4.** Sift together the flour, spices and salt, and reserve. **5.** Cool the water and soda mixture. **6.** Add eggs one at a time to the creamed mixture, beating well after each addition. **7.** Divide the combined flour and spices into four parts. Add this to the creamed mixture alternately with the cooled water-soda mixture, starting with flour and ending with flour. Stir well after each addition but do not beat. **8.** Follow preparation method for making butter cakes (page 9) and bake at 350°F for about 45 minutes. This recipe makes one square pan 9" x 9" x 2" deep.

A Shaker lemon pie with its meringue and ring of lemon slices makes a spectacular dessert.

P ies—foods enclosed in dough-like crusts—have been eaten
since ancient times. Pies were great favorites with the Shakers, for
they could be used with a variety of ingredients: meat, fruit, custards.
Two of Sister Jennie's favorites are presented here. One is a lemon pie,
different from the one made famous by Shakertown at Pleasant Hill,
Kentucky. The other is mincemeat, a pie with ancient origins. Mince
pie was eaten as a Christmas ritual in the England of long ago; made
of ingredients imported from the East, it symbolized the gifts of the
Wise Men to the infant Jesus.

Lemon Pie

Grate rind of one lemon
squeeze juice
take 1 cup sugar, yolks of two eggs
2 tablespoons flour
1 cup of water — boil all
in pail set inside kettle.
line pie tins with good crust,
prick and set in oven.

Lemon Pie

Sister Jennie's Lemon Pie is as tangy as any lemon pie enthusiast could ever want, and with a decorated meringue topping, it makes a spectacular dessert. Be warned, however: her old-fashioned lemon pie may not be as stiff as the starch-supported commercial stuff modern folk are used to.

1 1/2 cups sugar	Juice and grated rind of 2
1/4 teaspoon salt	lemons
3/4 cup flour	1 tablespoon butter
2 cups boiling water	2 thinly sliced lemons
4 egg yolks, room temperature	1/4 cup sugar

1. In the top of a double boiler, over hot water or in a saucepan over low heat, stir sugar, salt and flour. **2.** Add boiling water slowly, stirring constantly and rapidly. **3.** Cook until thickened, stirring as needed to prevent lumping. Mixture should thicken fairly quickly. **4.** When thickened, pour slowly, in a thin stream, over the egg yolks and stir vigorously. **5.** Add lemon juice, rind and butter, and return custard to boiler top. **6.** Place boiler top over hot water and continue cooking until yolks have thickened, about 5 to 8 minutes. **7.** Cool slightly, then pour into a baked 9″ pie shell (page 43) and chill. **8.** Top with meringue (directions below) when cooled. **9.** Sprinkle lemon slices with sugar and arrange on top of meringue, with slices slightly overlapping. **10.** Brown meringue in 425°F oven for 3 to 5 minutes.

Meringue Topping

4 egg whites	1/4 teaspoon cream of
1/4 teaspoon salt	tartar
	2/3 cup sugar

1. Beat egg whites with salt and cream of tartar until soft peaks are formed. **2.** Add sugar gradually, a little at a time, and continue beating until stiff, but not dry, peaks are formed. **3.** Spread on cooled pie; brown lightly in a moderately hot oven.

Mince Meat

---

6 Marble 23 lbs
2½ Sugar
4 Currants
3 Rasins
2 ℔ x.a Peel
½ " Citron
1½ " Butter Nuts
1½ " Valencea Almonds
{ Blanched
1¼ Crackers
1 oz Cinnamon
1 oz Ginger
1 oz Mace
Grate Rind & Tendrs
Juice of 3
4½ Apples
3 lbs old Cydar
1 ℔ any Dark Pres

Mince Pie

Authentic Shaker mincemeat takes time and patience, which may explain why Sister Jennie's original recipe yielded such a large amount. Our version is for a much smaller amount, but to enjoy it, you will still need to start planning months ahead.

1 1/4 cups sugar
3 cups currants
2 1/2 cups dark raisins
1 1/4 cups diced glazed
   mixed fruit
3/4 cup glazed citron, diced
1 1/2 cups pecans or walnut
   pieces
1/2 cup slivered almonds
2 cups crushed soda crackers
   without salted tops

1 tablespoon cinnamon
1/2 teaspoon salt
2 teaspoons grated nutmeg
Grated rind of 2 lemons
Juice of 1 lemon
4 cups diced tart apples, unpared
1/2 cup hard or sweet cider
1/2 cup brandy
1/2 cup grape wine or
   grape jelly

1. Mix all ingredients together for at least 15 minutes.   **2.** Pack into a *sterile* crock or jar.   **3.** Cover with paraffin or buttered brown paper. If paper is used, press on top of the mincemeat.   **4.** Cover tightly with a second piece of buttered brown paper or plasticized freezer paper, and tie around rim of jar or crock. Let ripen for 3 months in a cool, dry place. (Note: The alcohol preserves the product; fermentation will occur if none is used.)

All-Purpose Pastry

3/4 cup butter
3 cups sifted all-purpose flour

7 to 8 tablespoons ice water,
blended with 1/2 teaspoon salt

1. With a pastry blender, cut *half* of the butter into the flour until the mixture resembles coarse meal.   **2.** Cut remaining butter into the flour mixture until the butter particles are the size of small peas or beans.   **3.** With a two- or three-tined fork, toss in just enough ice water—a little at a time—until the mixture leaves the sides of the bowl in a ball. It is not necessary to use all the ice water.   **4.** Roll out to the desired thickness on a lightly floured board.

Shaker Plum Pudding from Sister Jennie's original recipe is a special treat for the holidays...or anytime.

Pudding

The origins of pudding are as ancient and humble as porridge or gruel, but by the time of the Shakers, puddings had become more elaborate, ranging from dessert puddings made with rice to the elegance of what is often called Christmas pudding. In their various ways puddings provided a change of pace from the succession of cakes, pies and cookies with which our ancestors fortified themselves. Christmas observances varied among the Shaker societies, but all regarded it as a day to be observed in a special way, with sacred music, a minimum of chores, and a dinner with, perhaps, a Christmas or plum pudding like this one.

Shaker Plum Pudding

1 tt Currents
1 tt Rasins
1 tt Sultana Rasins
1/2 " X Peel O.L.C
1/2 " Blanched Almonds
1/2 " Butter
1/2 " Butter Nuts
1/2 " Sugar
6 Eggs well beaten
1/2 ~~tt~~ Bread crumbs
Rind Grated 3 Lemons
Damp with New milk

Burn Sugar to Spoon to
darken pack in Basins
& Boil 3 Hours & 2 Hours
Tie Cloth well over Basin

46

Plum Pudding

Sister Jennie probably reserved this for special occasions.

1 cup each currants,
    raisins, white raisins
1/2 cup each candied citron
    or fruit, slivered almonds,
    pecans
1/4 teaspoon each, allspice
    and nutmeg

Rind of 1 lemon, grated
1/3 cup butter
1/2 cup dark brown sugar
2 eggs, well beaten
5 slices fresh bread,
    crumbed and soaked in
    1 1/4 cups milk

1. Mix all of the dried fruits and nuts with the spices and rind.   **2.** Cream the butter until light and fluffy.   **3.** Cream in the brown sugar to the butter until no lumps remain.   **4.** Beat in eggs to the creamed mixture and cream again, to incorporate air.   **5.** Stir in fruit and nuts.   **6.** Stir in soaked bread crumbs.   **7.** Pack mixture in a buttered 6-cup pudding baisin or 2 empty one-pound coffee cans. Be sure to tie buttered brown paper over the top of each container, or use a covered pudding mold.   **8.** Place containers on a rack in a large pot, taking care that simmering water not touch the pudding containers. Cover and steam for about 3 hours. Check water level each hour and replace if necessary.

Sauces

Lemon pie filling (page 41) makes a delicious sauce. Or you may prefer our more traditional Brandied Hard Sauce.

1/2 cup butter
2 to 3 cups powdered sugar

1 tablespoon brandy
    and 1 teaspoon dark rum

1. Cream the butter until creamy and fluffy.   **2.** Add the brandy and rum.   **3.** Cream again, adding powdered sugar a little at a time, until a stiff consistency is achieved. Some people like the sauce at a spreading consistency, while others prefer it stiff and almost crumbly. Use just enough sugar to achieve the desired result.   **4.** Pack into a bowl or jar. Cover and let ripen for a few hours in a refrigerator to blend flavors.

Contributors

This book is the work of many hands, seen and unseen. Some, such as the Shaker sisters and brothers who gave their recipes to Jennie Wells long ago, can never be identified. But they share credit with those who can.

Sister Jennie M. Wells collected the original recipes and recorded them in her notebook. Born in Buffalo, N.Y., on February 4, 1878, she entered Shaker life at the Watervliet, N.Y., society, then moved to Mt. Lebanon, N.Y., and finally to Hancock, Mass. She died in a nearby nursing home on January 11, 1956, age 77.

James H. Bissland Jr., the co-author's father, was a close friend of Sister Jennie and received the notebook as a gift from her. A graduate of the Massachusetts Institute of Technology and a professional engineer, he was a man of many talents and interests, and was acquainted with the Shakers for a number of years. He died in 1964.

James H. Bissland III, co-author, now owns Sister Jennie's original notebook. A member of the faculty of the School of Journalism of Bowling Green State University in Ohio, he coordinated and edited *Sister Jennie's Shaker Desserts.*

Arthur P. Tolve, the primary author of the published version of Sister Jennie's dessert recipes, made the selections from the much larger number available in the original notebook, then tested and refined them for modern cooks. A member of the faculty of the Department of Home Economics at Bowling Green State University, he teaches courses in restaurant and institutional food service management.

Lynn Bauman Hostetler designed this book and supervised its printing. A graphic designer in Bowling Green, Ohio, she is the art director for Bowling Green State University's public relations and publications office. She also tested the recipes.

Frank Breithaupt illustrated *Sister Jennie's Shaker Desserts* with his photographs. A graduate of the School of Journalism at Bowling Green State University, he is a prize-winning photojournalist with *The Journal,* Lorain, Ohio.

Don E. Bright, professor of business education at Bowling Green State University, conducted the third and final round of testing of the recipes. Cooking is his hobby.

Sarah K. Bissland, a granddaughter of the man who orginally received the recipes from Sister Jennie, proofread the printed text of the book. She is a wire copy editor for *The Journal,* Lorain, Ohio.

Sister Jennie's Shaker Desserts is set in Compugraphic Goudy Old Style throughout. The main text is in 12-point type, with recipe headings in 30 point. Sister Jennie's original recipes appear in her own handwriting. This book was printed by Fisher Printing Co., Galion, Ohio 44833, on 80-lb. Warren Olde Style text and 80-lb. Warren Lustro Enamel cover stock.